Contents

Prologue ....

1) Backpacking in Southeast Asia - An Introductio

  1.1 Why Southeast Asia?..5

  1.2 Snapshot Country Summaries.......................................6

2) Things to do before your Trip 12

  2.1 Get any necessary Vaccinations and Malaria tablets 12

  2.2 Get Travel Insurance 13

  2.3 Book a Flight to Southeast Asia..................................14

  2.4 Get a Backpack and pack 14

  2.5 Do some Planning and Background Research.........................16

3) Suggested Backpacking Routes.......................................18

  3.1 PART 1 - Thai Islands, Beaches & Parties 18

  3.2 PART 2 - Southeast Asia Mainland Loop 22

  3.3 PART 3 - The Philippines..29

  3.4 PART 4 - Indonesia 31

  3.5 Myanmar...33

  3.6 The Best of the Rest 36

4) Visas & Border Crossings 38

  4.1 Entry Requirements 38

  4.2 Border Crossings 41

5) Budgeting..47

  5.1 Money 47

  5.2 Typical Backpacking Costs in Southeast Asia 50

6) Best Festivals...54

7) Where to Party...59

  7.1 Top 10 Party Destinations 59

7.2 Full Moon Parties 61

8) Top 10 Places to Experience Local Culture 65

9) Best Destinations for Adventure & Nature 69

9.1 Five Activities for Active Travellers & Adrenaline Junkies 69

9.2 Five Natural Wonders 70

10) First Timers in Southeast Asia – FAQs 73

11) About 80

11.1 About Funky Guides 80

11.2 About this Guide 80

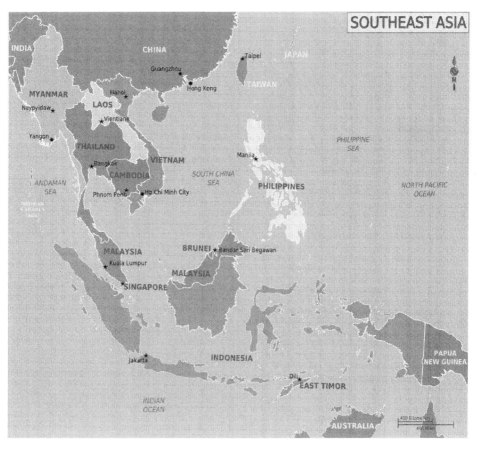

Prologue

Welcome to Bangkok, Death to Drug Traffickers

This is the cheerful warning that often greets new arrivals at Bangkok's Suvarnabhumi Airport. It might be on the visitor arrivals forms or if you're particularly lucky it might just be hovering above the luggage carousel as you anxiously wait for your backpack to show up. The welcome is actually comparatively tame when compared to those issued out in neighbouring countries such as Indonesia which spices things up with the image of a loaded gun or Malaysia which favours the noose. Either way it's an intimidating welcome to what is on the whole an incredibly peaceful if contradictory region.

Bangkok is the main flight hub in this part of the world and it is where most Southeast Asian adventures begin and end. This giant city of sin can be the making or breaking of anyone who falls under its spell. Many shudder at the mere mention of the word while others are taken in by its undeniable buzz. It is the pulsating heart of the region and in the middle of it all is Khao San Road, the centre of the backpacking universe and base for almost every budget-minded traveller in the city.

That first jetlagged stroll down Khao San can be another intimidating experience, especially if you arrive after dark when the shifty salesmen and promo girls are out in force and the hordes of travelling drunks are just gearing up for another night of excess. While it may be your first experience of Asia, the number of young European faces, Australian accents, fast-food chains and bars playing American music over the sight of English football are likely to offer up an immediate reminder of home. While there is much, much more to Bangkok than Khao San Road and its neighbouring streets and narrow alleyways, it is at least a very useful base for those first footsteps on Southeast Asian soil. Rest assured that whatever you need or wherever you want to go, it won't take long before someone offers to help you (for a price, of course).

Almost anything goes in the Thai capital yet nothing is ever quite as it seems. Bent cops share the streets with ladyboys, poverty surrounds palaces and middle-aged white men walk hand in hand with teenaged Thai girls. With almost anything you could possibly want and plenty more you wouldn't for sale, it won't be long before you realise that you 'ain't in Kansas no more'. Fortunately though Southeast Asia has its very own ready-made Yellow Brick Road AKA 'The Banana Pancake trail' to follow. Along the way you'll meet all kinds of weirdos, drunks, hippies, tricksters and plenty of morons but will probably end up having lots of fun. Veer off it every now and then, and you might just find what you really came for.

1) Backpacking in Southeast Asia - An Introduction

1.1 Why Southeast Asia?

These days a backpacking trip to Southeast Asia almost seems to be a rites of passage for 18-30 year olds from countries like Britain, Germany, Canada and Australia. Southeast Asia continues to attract hundreds of thousands of budget travellers each year, far more than any other region.

Why is it so popular with a primarily youthful crowd of westerners? The answers to this question haven't really changed in decades even if the experience itself certainly has. We could split the answer into four fairly generalised parts:

1) Culture & History

Southeast Asia with its mystical temples, Buddhist beliefs, remote tribes and special customs continues to intrigue and mystify those from other parts of the world. Its ways are completely unique even compared to neighbouring regions in Asia and each of its countries has its own way of doing things. The cultural aspect was certainly what first attracted travellers to this region and despite globalisation and an influx of foreigners, ancient practices are still very much alive in large parts of Southeast Asia.

As far as the world's major religions go, Buddhism is generally considered to be 'the cool one' and spending time learning about it in a predominantly Buddhist region is another big draw. Don't be surprised if you go home a casual Buddhist!

2) Adventure Sports, Jungle Treks, Deep Sea Dives, Mountain Hikes etc.

The active traveller is drawn to Southeast Asia's jungles, mountains, oceans, rivers and waterfalls. All kinds of weird and wonderful adventure sports have developed over the years and are on offer for bargain prices. Whether you want to learn to scuba-dive, climb volcanoes or raft down furious rapids you'll be able to find a little corner of Southeast Asia that suits you just fine. If you're not into the adrenaline junkie stuff then there are lots of opportunities to experience natural wonders at a more tranquil pace too.

3) Chilling out on beaches & Partying

For some reason these two seem to go hand in hand. Southeast Asia is home to gorgeous beaches and islands, clear warm waters and year-round sunshine so for beach bums it's basically a paradise where you could spend weeks, perhaps even months just island hopping and relaxing. By night there are beach parties on all the main Thai islands and a few other beaches in the region and the wild backpacker party culture that has developed sucks in many who find it difficult to leave behind.

4) It's very cheap!

These days most travellers tend to combine each of the other three aspects into one trip although perhaps lean more towards one than the other two depending on their interests. They have one unifying factor though that contributes a great deal to the region's popularity. Visitors from most countries will find Southeast Asia extremely cheap. Lengthy trips of several months or more are possible for anyone who has managed to save up a bit of cash. More on this later!

1.2 Snapshot Country Summaries

Thailand

By some distance the most popular country in the region in terms of visitor numbers. Almost every single backpacker in Southeast Asia visits Thailand and most start there. Very loosely speaking you could divide it into two main regions with Bangkok as the connecting piece. The south and its many offshore islands are home to some of the world's best beaches and two or three of the islands have developed a crazy party scene.

If you want something a bit more traditional it's best to head in the opposite direction from the capital and make your way up North. Chiang Mai is the cultural epicentre and although the backpacker trail has very much landed here too, there are plenty of ways to get a more authentic experience of life in Thailand, in and around the city and in other parts of Northern Thailand.

Cambodia

While it's too simplistic to say Cambodia is what Thailand used to be like, it is far less commercialised and more primitive than its larger neighbour. It is home to the best temple complex in the region and perhaps the world (Angkor Wat), certainly one of the highlights of any visit to Southeast Asia.

The other major although rather more morbid 'attractions' are sites such as the Killing Fields and Tuol Sleng Prison in the capital Phnom Penh, which document in a shockingly real way the tragedies of the Cambodian Genocide in the 1970's. You could probably add to the bizarre mix, the hedonistic and often drug-fuelled backpacker nightlife scene that can be found in a few places and you have the main reasons why travellers come to Cambodia.

Vietnam

To people of older generations Vietnam is still talked about as though it is a war rather than a country. Anyone who actually visits will discover there is a whole lot more to the place even if the scars haven't completely disappeared.

It may surprise you to know that there are more people in Vietnam than in Thailand, Laos and Cambodia combined and if you're just doing the typical mainland Southeast Asia trail, it's perhaps the easiest place to observe and interact with locals and learn about their way of life. The cities are hectic bustling places and although it is still a Communist country, business is booming.

Just travelling from A to B is a thrill here and whether you get a cheap motorbike and explore the country or settle for the famous Reunification express train-line, which connects the capital Hanoi in the North with the larger Ho Chi Minh City in the South, it is sure to be an unforgettable experience.

Laos

In total contrast to much of neighbouring Vietnam where the pace of life is often frenetic, Laos is renowned for its laid back lifestyle. Even the main cities are little more than sleepy towns and villages. Nothing happens quickly in Laos. When you're trying to get around that can be frustrating but when you're watching the sun set over the Mekong River with an ice cold Beer Lao it's not so bad.

As far as typical backpacker activities go, well there are loads of beautiful temples (almost a given in Southeast Asia) to visit while the Elephant Sanctuary lets you meet rescued elephants which at the very least will provide you with a new profile picture (until you visit the Tiger Kingdom in Thailand!). Then there is tubing, one of the iconic images of backpacking in Southeast Asia. It combines the most popular backpacker hobby (drinking) with lazing about on a rubber ring in a river, which is fun too. Brilliant idea, only it can be very dangerous and fatalities are not uncommon. The authorities have massively cracked down on it in recent years but it's still good fun and Vang Vieng remains one of the main backpacker hubs in the country.

There is also a sad side to Laos, which is the most heavily bombed country, per capita, in the history of the world. There are still an estimated 80 million unexploded US bombs littered around the country today and there are several sites where you can learn about the damage this continues to inflict on the Lao people and the efforts being made to deal with the problem.

Myanmar (Burma)

Until very recently Burma wasn't even an option for travellers in Southeast Asia with limited flights in, closed borders and strict visa rules but things are slowly changing and this one time pariah state is gradually opening its doors.

There are thousands of years' worth of history to be discovered here and its relative isolation adds to its sense of mystique and adventure. Travel can be slow and frustrating and there's nowhere near the amount of budget accommodation options that you'll find elsewhere so it's not as cheap as you might think. Highlights include the stunning Inle Lake, home to floating village communities, Bagan and its pagodas (there are thousands of them) and the cities of Mandalay and Yangon.

However even since the rise to power of the iconic Aung San Suu Kyi in 2016, human rights abuses, particularly regarding the persecution of the country's Rohingya Muslim minority have continued and according to some reports have got far worse. As a result there are certainly moral question-marks as to whether or not to visit the country.

Malaysia

Unlike the predominantly Buddhist states to the North, Malaysia is an Islamic country although religious freedom is written into their constitution. It is clearly divided into two main regions, with half of the country bordering Thailand and Singapore on the mainland and the other half consisting of part of the huge island of Borneo which it shares with Indonesia and Brunei.

The mainland section is noticeably more modern and better organised than other countries in Southeast Asia and there's plenty in and around cities like Kuala Lumpur and Penang to keep you entertained. If you're looking for its wild side then head to Borneo which is far less developed and almost resembles a different country altogether. Like Thailand it has plenty of small but stunning islands although without the hedonistic party element.

Singapore

The city state of Singapore is incomparable to the rest of the region with its glitzy modern skyscrapers and fancy marinas. It's not a budget travel paradise by any means and certainly isn't the place get drunk and go crazy given that alcohol is extremely expensive even by Western standards and laws are certainly on the strict side. Depending on what you read, anything from forgetting to flush the toilet, expressing Atheist beliefs or public hugging can land you in trouble with the law here but it's not quite the cold-hearted, business-orientated, police state that it's often presented as.

It has a fascinating and diverse history which has left it as one of the most multicultural cities on the planet with Chinese, British, Indian and Malay influences all very evident. There are lots of fascinating districts to explore and it has excellent flight connections so it's easy to fit into your trip.

Indonesia

18,110. That's the number of islands that make up Indonesia. If you visited one new island every day, it would take you 49 years and 213 days to get through them all. What we're getting at here is that Indonesia is a really big place and unless you've got nothing better to do for the next 50 years of your life it's basically impossible to see it all so you need to pick and choose which parts you visit.

Some of the main islands include Java, the heart and soul of the country where over half of Indonesians live. It's home to several of the most active volcanoes in the world which make for some exciting if somewhat dangerous trips. Moving east you get to Bali, Indonesia's biggest backpacking destination and the only place in the country with large numbers of travellers. Lombok, Flores, Sumatra and Borneo are other islands you might want to consider in a country where it's easier to get 'off the beaten track' because away from a few islands, the track barely even exists.

The Philippines

Misunderstood and absent from many Southeast Asian backpacking itineraries is The Philippines, which is also made up of a large collection of islands, although most are quite small. There are several major differences that sets them apart from Indonesia and mainland Southeast Asia.

Firstly a large Spanish heritage has given the islands a Latin flair and a passionate brand of Catholicism. Yet it is English and not Spanish that is one of the two official languages here which certainly makes travelling a lot easier. Travellers with a thirst for adventure sports will feel right at home here while sun-seekers will love what are certainly the best beaches in Southeast Asia outside of Thailand. The chirpy Filipinos will probably tell you that their beaches are superior and they have a strong case.

One thing that puts some visitors off is the country's dangerous reputation and trigger-happy president Rodrigo Duterte's extrajudicial killings have been creating international headlines. Anyone who gets involved in drugs here risks being killed, while some areas are also a hotbed of criminal activity including both Muslim and Christian areas of Mindanao. The situation can be volatile so check for updates at the time you travel.

2) Things to do before your Trip

2.1 Get any necessary Vaccinations and Malaria tablets

This is something you should do at least a month, perhaps even several months before your trip as it takes time for the vaccinations and tablets to kick into effect. Getting sick in Southeast Asia really isn't much fun. In most of the region healthcare services fall well short of a decent standard and the few places that provide good healthcare charge extortionate fees. Therefore take the necessary precautions before you go.

Head down to your local doctor's surgery or health centre and tell them where you're planning on going and for how long and they should be able to provide you with a list of recommended vaccinations. If the list is long then consider talking to a couple of other sources in the health industry and see if it is really necessary to have them all. Opinions do tend to vary wildly between health professionals about what is absolutely necessary and what is little more than an expensive waste of time.

As a guideline travellers tend to have as a minimum vaccinations against the following diseases:

Hepatitis A

Hepatitis B

Typhoid

Diphtheria / Tetanus / Polio (Combined into 1 shot)

You may find that you have already had some of these vaccinations when you were younger and may still be protected.

Malaria is extremely prevalent in some parts of Cambodia, Laos and Myanmar and several areas of Thailand that border those countries although the situation does seem to be improving. There is a low risk in parts of Vietnam and Malaysia, while the risk is high on a few of the main Indonesian islands. Only Africa has a bigger Malaria problem than Southeast Asia so precautions are important as it is a deadly disease.

There are several different drugs available although some of them only work effectively in certain parts of Southeast Asia as resistance has built up so you may need more than one prescription. Talk to a health professional and tell them about all the areas you may visit and they should be able to suggest the most effective tablets. It is equally important, even if you are on malaria pills, that you take precautions to avoid bites where possible when you're on the road and try to stay in places with mosquito nets over the beds in high-risk areas.

There is more information and current maps on the risk of malaria and other diseases in individual countries here - www.fitfortravel.nhs.uk/destinations/asia-(east).aspx

2.2 Get Travel Insurance

Getting insurance that covers you against the sort of things that can go wrong in Southeast Asia is also important. Travel insurance for a backpacking trip is very different from typical holiday insurance. This is because the trips tend to be much longer, often including visits to quite primitive destinations and perhaps including a range of potentially dangerous activities. These kind of things are often not included in regular travel insurance packages so it is important to carefully check what is covered before you book anything.

It can be an expensive purchase but it can also save you thousands in the unlikely event of something going badly wrong while you're in Asia. There are only a few companies that really specialise in providing cover for backpackers. We recommend World Nomads (www.worldnomads.com).

2.3 Book a Flight to Southeast Asia

The main question here is whether to book a return flight or whether to just get a single ticket. If you have a strict timeframe, limited funds or something you need to return home for then it makes sense money-wise to get a return but otherwise getting just a single offers you a lot more flexibility.

From Europe, flights to Bangkok are generally the cheapest with London, Amsterdam and Frankfurt amongst the best places to fly from. There are also numerous airlines offering flights from Europe to Bangkok via cities like Abu Dhabi, Doha and Muscat in the Middle East and the distance involved will probably require you to change flights. From Australia and New Zealand you can get good deals on flights to Indonesia or Singapore and then work your way north. From North America and certainly the West Coast it should be quicker to fly across the Pacific. Consider visiting the Philippines first as this is closest.

Use a flight comparison site like Skyscanner (www.skyscanner.com) or Fare Compare (www.farecompare.com) to hunt down the cheapest fares. If you're flexible about the dates and book a month or more in advance you can usually find a good price. If you're a student or under 26 (or even if you're not) have a look at Sta Travel (www.statravel.com) as they often have special deals on flights to and from the region and they also offer multiflex passes which give you the option to change your dates after you've booked, which is handy for these kind of long trips.

2.4 Get a Backpack and pack

Getting a good backpack that is sturdy and most importantly you are comfortable with, is very important as you are going to be living out of it and carrying it everywhere for the duration of your trip. Shop around, visit a few places (camping stores are a good starting point) and try lots of backpacks on your back. Remember it will be considerably heavier when you have packed it. It needs to be strong, waterproof and of good enough quality that it won't break but not to the point where you can't carry the damn thing.

When it comes to packing don't fall for the cardinal sin that first-time backpackers often make which is packing far too much. You need only the essentials and anything you really feel you can't live without. There are shops and laundry services in Southeast Asia too! If you realise you have forgotten something or need to buy something then just get it while you're out there.

Once you've packed, consider walking around your garden or your street with your backpack on and see how it feels. You're going to be doing a lot of that in the months to come and probably in much hotter, humid conditions. If it feels too heavy now you've probably packed too much and there should always be some space at the top of your bag for things you buy on the road. Also remember that often you won't have time to neatly pack everything while you are travelling so if it's a struggle to fit everything in now, it will become a major pain when you are away.

Items such as mobile phones and laptops aren't essential by any means but almost everybody takes a mobile and it does at least allow you to keep in touch with people at home more easily. Almost every hostel has Wi-Fi although the quality varies. Some backpackers take laptops or tablets but unless you have a specific reason for doing so, it's not really necessary and there are internet cafes everywhere. If you take expensive electronic items then it's worth forking out to stay in slightly better places that are more secure and certainly don't stay in dorms that don't have lockers.

Below is a basic checklist of things you should be packing:

Money - some emergency cash (US Dollars are most useful) and preferably at least two other sources of money in case you have problems with debit cards etc. Keep one in your wallet/purse and one in your backpack, so you will always have a back-up if you're unfortunate enough to lose one or have it stolen.

Documents - passport, flight tickets, photocopy of your passport, record of any vaccinations you've had, a few passport sized photos, travel insurance confirmation.

Clothes - 7-10 days' worth of casual clothes suitable for hot weather and perhaps one or two warmer things if you end up somewhere a bit cooler.

Swimwear and towels - 2 sets of swimwear unless you don't plan on spending much time on the beach. 2 preferably light-weight towels would also be sensible as they aren't usually provided in hostels and you'll want one for the beach and another one for showering.

Shoes - lightweight flip-flops and perhaps another pair of shoes for general use and a pair of trainers or boots if you are planning more active things.

Toiletries - just bare essentials like toothpaste, toothbrush, and shower gel. Buy more when you run out.

First aid - plasters, sun protection, diarrhoea pills, headache tablets, malaria tablets, contraception.

Small lock - important. Perhaps take two, one for you bag and one for your locker.

Earplugs - very handy if you are planning on staying in noisy dorms.

Mp3 player, headphones & charger - lifesaver on long journeys.

power adaptor - you can get worldwide one's quite cheap these days and they are your best option as the type of sockets vary between countries and sometimes even between different cities in the same country.

2.5 Do some Planning and Background Research

Don't plan your entire trip out day by day as your plans will very quickly fall apart when you start travelling. However as a minimum you should have at least a basic idea of the places you want to visit and how much time you have for your trip. The next section should help you decide this and give you an indication as to what a realistic timeframe might be for all you want to see.

Research whether or not you will need a visa and how long a stay you will be granted for each country that you are considering visiting. Depending on your nationality the answer varies. This doesn't necessarily mean you have to get your visa(s) now as it's often better to sort it out in Southeast Asia and most countries now offer some form of visa on arrival. More on this is in Section 4.

The other major consideration is money. You want to leave home comfortable in the knowledge that you aren't going to run out of cash before the end of your trip. It's useful to have a rough idea of typical backpacking expenses in the countries you're thinking of visiting. Section 5 on budgeting should help with this and you can use it to set a budget for your trip or decide if your intended budget is going to be enough.

3) Suggested Backpacking Routes

Remember that bit about veering off the banana pancake trail? If the answer is no go back to the first page and read it! If the answer is yes things are about to get a little hypocritical. Well sort of. This suggested route more or less follows that well-trodden trail in mainland Southeast Asia. However you don't need to follow this like a confused blind puppy. It's there as a guideline and only that.

As well as the mainland Southeast Asia route included are itineraries for the large island nations of Indonesia and The Philippines and connection suggestions. Indonesia (Kuta beach in Bali aside) and to an even greater extent The Philippines are far removed from the standard South East Asian backpacking routes but both have so much to offer it is a wonder why. There is also a route for Myanmar, which is becoming easier and more popular to visit.

For convenience reasons the main route has been split into separate chunks but if you have got about 5 months free then you can easily do it as one big trip. If not then pick and choose which parts appeal most. If you love the idea of chilling out on the beach and partying till dawn then Part 1 is essential. Part 2 is the longest and takes in a fairly common loop including the best that Northern Thailand, Laos, Vietnam and Cambodia has to offer. Parts 3 and 4 are all about island hopping and adventure in The Philippines and Indonesia.

Getting in and out of Myanmar isn't as simple as land border crossings are few and far between so we've treated the Myanmar route as separate to the main one (Parts 1-4) but there are suggestions of how to fit it in. For each destination there is also a suggested amount of time to spend there and a recommended budget hostel.

3.1 PART 1 - Thai Islands, Beaches & Parties

time : 3-4 weeks

comfortable backpacker budget : $1000 | 35,000 Thai Baht

shoestring budget : $650 | 23,000 Thai Baht

This is party central and how much you spend will depend a lot on how much alcohol you drink. You won't get by on the shoestring budget if you are out partying every night. The comfortable backpacker budget allows for a fair amount of drunken shenanigans but not partying hard every single night and still doing excursions in the day so if that sounds like you, you may wish to allow for a bit more even still.

Bangkok (2/3 days)

Some people love Bangkok, some hate it. There are a few sights worth seeing so take a few days to get over the jetlag and get used to Thailand before heading south. You'll need to come back later on so there will be another chance to see more of the city if you want to.

suggested accommodation: Born Free Hostel, Samsen Soi 6

This is near Khao San Road which is a huge backpacker area. For your first night or two though it might be an idea to get a private room to get over the tiredness and jetlag as hostel dorms in Southeast Asia aren't the best places to catch some sleep.

Phuket (2/3 days)

Phuket is touristy and attracts a wealthier bunch of tourists than the following places but it has some great beaches. The nightlife is quite sleazy in the main resort towns, especially Patong so don't go crazy here as the islands are better and more budget friendly places to party.

suggested accommodation: Sea Blue Phuket Hostel, 74/11 Soi Banzaan, Nanai Rd, Patong Beach

Koh Phi Phi (4/5 days)

Despite a heavy influx of visitors, the Phi Phi Islands are still absolutely beautiful and Phi Phi Don has a buzzing backpacker vibe and insane party scene. From there you can organise trips out to the surrounding islands, including Maya Bay, where the movie 'The Beach' was set.

suggested accommodation: Centerpoint Hostel, 179/16 Moo 7

The standard of budget accommodation is very low here. Centerpoint is an unremarkable, no frills hostel but at 250 Baht for a bed in a 6 bed dorm, it's about as cheap as you are likely to find in Phi Phi town and as the name suggests is in the centre of all the action. Don't expect to get any sleep before 2:00am though and be sure to check the rooftop Banana Bar over the road, which has a bit of a Bob Marley vibe if you get our drift, while the bar on the corner right next to the hostel has a live band every night and gradually develops into a cracking sing-a-long, dance-a-long party most nights.

If you fancy something quieter then there are plenty of beach bungalows but you might have to do a fair bit of walking to find the cheaper ones.

Railay Beach, Krabi (2/3 days)

Back on the mainland, Krabi is a nice place to get a beach bungalow for rock bottom prices and chill out. The main backpacker beach is Railay, which is only accessible by boat from Ao Nang or Krabi Town and is a bit of a hub for adventure sports with rock-climbing very popular.

suggested accommodation: Railay Cabana Bungalows, Railay Beach

These can be as low as 100 baht in the off-season. Get a boat to Railay Beach and it's a 10 minute walk uphill to Cabana Bungalows. Ask for directions, it's a small place on Rai Leh East.

Koh Tao (4/5 days)

This is the first of the three main islands in the Gulf of Thailand. It's the smallest and most relaxing of the trio but there are also some decent fire-themed beach parties every night. The most popular activity here is diving and many travellers opt to do a course which enables you to get a full diving qualification. You can book this on the island or in advance.

suggested accommodation: Good Dream Hostel, 15/19 Moo. 1, Sairee Beach

Again this is a nice place to stay in a beach bungalow. If you plan on staying for a while then maybe check into a hostel for a couple of days and try to find people willing to share a bungalow. Accommodation is also included with some of the diving courses.

Koh Phangan (5-7 days)

This is where the famous full moon parties happen and it's worth timing your trip to arrive here several days before full moon. There are lots of pool parties and jungle parties in the run up to the main night and these parties can be even better than the full moon party on the beach. There are black moon and half-moon parties too which have a slightly different vibe and many people find them more appealing than the main event. Check Section 7 for party dates. The parties aside there is plenty to do on Koh Phangan and the Northern part of the island is where you can escape the crowds, get rock bottom prices and find more active things to do.

suggested accommodation: Echo Beach Backpackers, 30 Moo 1, Baan Tai Beach

If you come for full moon then booking accommodation in advance is important. Otherwise it should be plentiful.

Koh Samui (2/3 days)

The biggest and most touristy of the islands. It is less popular with budget travellers so either stay for a few days if you want some more beach time or skip it altogether and move on to the next part of your trip.

suggested accommodation: Ananas Samui Hostel, 103/13 Moo 2, T. Maret

CONNECTION - You will probably need to head back to Bangkok for onward connections if you are following Part 2 of the route or going to most other places in the region or beyond. You can do this by a combination of boats, buses and/or trains. If you're feeling lazy you can fly from Koh Samui. Often there isn't much of a price difference.

Note domestic flights go to Bangkok's Don Mueang Airport rather than Suvarnabhumi, the main international airport.

3.2 PART 2 - Southeast Asia Mainland Loop

time : 8 - 10 weeks

comfortable backpacker budget : $2000

shoestring budget : $1500

THAILAND

Bangkok (1/2 days)

Spend a day or two more in Bangkok or move straight on. It's a good place to buy anything you need or have run out of, as the choice in Cambodia isn't anywhere near as wide.

suggested accommodation: Born Free Hostel, Samsen Soi 6

CAMBODIA

Siem Reap (4 days)

The main reason why travellers come to Siem Reap or indeed why the town exists at all are the fabulous Temples of Angkor Wat. Easily the most impressive temples in the region and set in dense jungle, it feels like a real adventure discovering them. There are loads of temples over a large area so it is best to take a couple of days to explore them. Siem Reap itself has a really chilled night market and a lively traveller party scene has developed along the imaginatively named Pub Street. You can also explore the giant Tonle Sap Lake area from here. It is home to river communities and lots of wildlife including crocodiles, leopards, turtles and snakes.

suggested accommodation: Hostel Salakamreuk, Sala Lodge Road, Sangkat Salakamreuk

If you get a tuk-tuk from the bus station the driver may try to take you to a

hostel of his choice (i.e. one where he has a deal with the owners that brings him commission). This is fairly common practice in Cambodia and some other parts of the region. Insist on the hostel you want to go to or ask to be dropped off at Pub Street.

Battambang (2 days)

A quiet town on the Mekong River. Options here include volunteering to help the local communities and trekking or cycling to sites around the town. You can also take a nice boat ride down the Mekong in from Siem Reap which is pleasant given the next couple of months will all be primarily about buses and trains.

suggested accommodation: Ganesha Family Guesthouse, Street 1.5, 20 Ouk Saphea Commune, Svay Por Village

Phnom Penh (3/4 days)

This is a fairly peaceful capital city with many stunning temples and palaces but also a great deal of poverty. It is truly a city of contradictions that has the ability to both amaze and shock at the same time. This is also where the Killing Fields are (just outside of town) and there is a former prison (now a museum) in town where you can learn about the Cambodian Genocide.

suggested accommodation: Hostel Nomads, 89 St. 108

Sihanoukville (2/3 days)

Cambodia's most well-known beach destination and a great place to party. There are 24 hour bars here and it's an 'anything goes' party place with lots of backpackers. It's more crowded these days so if you just want to relax, it's probably best to head to Koh Rong or base yourself away from the main drag.

suggested accommodation: The Led Zephyr, Serendipity Beach Road, Sangkat 4

Koh Rong (2/3 days)

25km off the coast from Sihanoukville, Koh Rong is Cambodia's 2nd largest island. This is what the Thai islands might have once been like before commercialisation set in. The vibe is very chilled and it's the perfect place to spend aimless days relaxing and exploring its long, sandy shores. You may need to head back to Phnom Penh for an onward bus to Vietnam.

suggested accommodation: Vagabonds, opposite the koh rong backpackers pier

VIETNAM

Ho Chi Minh City (3/4 days)

Saigon or Ho Chi Minh City as it is now called, is one of the largest cities in Southeast Asia and the streets are crammed full of motorbikes. There are a few interesting if slightly biased museums and sites relating to the Vietnam War while the Pham Ngu Lao area is Vietnam's biggest backpacker district with lots of cheap hostels, restaurants and bars. HCMC is a little bit crazy and well worth a visit although unless you're a city lover you may find it somewhat overwhelming.

suggested accommodation: Vietnam Inn, 200 LeLai.st, BenThanh ward

Ask the taxi or moto-taxi driver to take you to Pham Ngu Lao and then ask for directions to Vietnam Inn or choose one of the many budget places in the area.

Mui Ne (2/3 days)

Gorgeous long beach and sand dunes. It's very quiet and the perfect place to relax after HCMC. Mui Ne is basically one long road which hugs the beach and everything is on it. It's a long way from one end to the other (about 20km) so you are slightly restricted at night by the location of your accommodation but it's not really a nightlife place anyway.

suggested accommodation: Mui Ne Backpacker Village, 137 Nguyen Dinh Chieu

Mui Ne is somewhere you may want to think about booking or at least researching some accommodation in advance. It's the not the sort of place where you can just get off the bus and find somewhere as the budget places are really spread out so you might end up walking for miles.

Da Lat (2/3 days)

This mountain town has a very different vibe from the rest of the country. The climate is much fresher and it can get quite chilly. It's a good place for hiking, biking and canyoning and there also some opportunities to meet locals and learn about their culture.

suggested accommodation: Backpackers Paradise, Lot D58 Hoang Van Thu, Ward 4

Nha Trang (2 days)

This is Vietnam's main beach resort but while it almost rivals the seediness of resorts in Thailand it is nowhere as nice. It's a big water sports centre popular with kite-surfers and there is a really nice temple with a giant Buddha statue that's worth a visit on the outskirts of the town.

suggested accommodation: Mojzo Inn, 120/36 Nguyen Thien Thuat St

Hoi An (3 days)

This a very popular spot with travellers in Central Vietnam and with 2000 years of history it's a pretty incredible place to learn about Vietnamese culture. The beautifully preserved centre has a 'stepping back in time' feel to it but it's still a thriving trading town and there is also a great beach nearby if you want to relax.

suggested accommodation: Hoa Binh Hotel, 696 Hai Ba Trung St

Hue (1/2 days)

Traditional riverside Vietnamese city. Not a great deal to see besides an ancient palace complex that has seen better days but it breaks up the journey and has a small backpacker district with some decent budget bars and excellent local cuisine.

suggested accommodation: Tigon Hostel, 11B Nguyen Cong Tru Street,

Ninh Binh (2 days)

The Tam Coc caves nearby are the main attraction and the surrounding countryside is very beautiful. You have now truly arrived in North Vietnam and should notice the difference fairly quickly. The town itself is not at all touristy and is memorable only because the people are incredibly friendly and as a foreigner you will constantly be greeted by people welcoming you to their town.

suggested accommodation: Tam Coc Backpacker Hostel, Van Lam, Ninh Hai

Halong Bay (3/4 days)

Halong Bay is one of the most beautiful spots in all of Southeast Asia. Choose an island to stay at (Cat Ba is a decent base) and then take a boat trip around the bay which is home to hundreds of incredible limestone islets.

suggested accommodation: Mr. ZOOM Backpacker Hostel, 25 Nui Ngoc, Cat Ba

Hanoi (3/4 days)

The Vietnamese capital. Loads of history and sites relating to the war and a lively old town which is where most travellers tend to stay. The city is built around lots of lakes and it still has a French feel to it thanks to its colonial past. Travellers tend to prefer Hanoi to HCMC which is bigger and more commercialised.

suggested accommodation: Hanoi Rendezvous Hostel, 27 Bat Dan, Hoan Kiem

CONNECTION - Hanoi to Vientiane (approx. $70 flight with Vietnam Airlines). If you're feeling brave you can do this overland but it's a 20 hour bus ride and not a particularly comfortable one.

. LAOS

Vientiane (3 days)

Vientiane is one of the most chilled out capitals on the planet. There are several beautiful temples and palaces worth checking out and be sure to visit COPE which documents the country's struggles against UXOs and provides valuable help to amputees. The city is nicely set looking over the Mekong River which separates Vientiane from Thailand.

suggested accommodation: Backpackers Garden Hostel, 028 Sihome Road

Vang Vieng (2/3 days)

This place used to be one of the biggest party destinations in SE Asia thanks to its tubing and wild riverside bars. You can still go tubing and there are still a few bars along the river to stop at but there has been a big crackdown on the drinking aspect as there were lots of injuries and some figures quote an alarming 20-30 backpacker deaths per year. The danger hasn't been completely removed and jumping in the water is a very bad idea as there are many sharp rocks just below the surface.

suggested accommodation: Easy Go Hostel, Wat That

Luang Prabang (3/4 days)

The nicest city in Laos with a great old quarter and beautiful temples. Outside of town there is so much to do. Trekking, biking and kayaking opportunities are on the menu as well as an elephant sanctuary which is popular with backpackers.

suggested accommodation: Central Backpackers Hostel, Noradeth road

THAILAND

Chiang Khong (2/3 days)

Right on the border with Laos, it is in the Golden Triangle, a famous opium growing region which covers areas of Thailand, Laos and Myanmar. It's a fascinating part of the world, home to many unique tribes and feels a world away from the mania of Bangkok and the islands in the South.

suggested accommodation: Baanrimtaling Home Stay, 19 Tesacan

Chiang Mai (4/5 days)

The main city in Northern Thailand and probably the best place in the country to really get to know Thai culture. You can study traditional Thai practices such as massage and meditation. It is also a great base for exploring or trekking into the jungle and checking out ethnic minority villages near the city.

suggested accommodation: Baan Arlhan, 18 Samlan Road Lane, 7 A T.Prasing

Pai (3/4 days)

This is a real traveller favourite. The town itself is set in a picturesque valley and has a major hippie vibe to it. It's a good place for adventure activities like zip-lining, elephant treks, tubing and rafting which are done in the surrounding land but can be arranged in Pai. You will probably need to head back to Chiang Mai before moving south.

suggested accommodation: KK.HUT, 313 M.1 T.Maehee, A.Pai Maehongson

Kamphaeng Phet (1 day)

Breaks up the train journey between Chiang Mai and Bangkok. Pleasant ancient town in a rarely visited part of Thailand.

suggested accommodation: 3 J Guesthouse, 79 Rachavitee Rd

Ayutthaya (1/2 days)

Ancient city with lots of history and old temples to take in. Consider renting a bike out (very cheap) and cycling around it. Just try not to collide with any of the peculiar and rather large lizard like creatures that roam ominously around parts of town.

suggested accommodation: Early Bird Hostel, 7/25 Pa Maphrao Rd

Bangkok (1/2 days)

Stock up on anything you need and do anything you haven't done yet in Bangkok. It's time to say goodbye to the Khao San Road and get ready for The Philippines! (or fly home if you are ending your trip here).

suggested accommodation: Born Free Hostel, Samsen Soi 6

CONNECTION - Direct flights from Bangkok to Manila do exist but are quite expensive. It's generally cheaper to fly to Kuala Lumpur or Singapore and then onto the Philippines. You can get to Manila for about $100 (plus any baggage fees) this way and obviously have the option of visiting somewhere new along the way. From Manila, you can fly to Kalibo International (from around $30), *which is close to Boracay, the first stop on the Filipino part of the route. Manila is a large city and a bit rough so it's probably better to go straight to Kalibo rather than hanging around there. You may need to return to Manila at the end of your time in The Philippines and it's easier to deal with once you've got more of a feel for the country.*

3.3 PART 3 - The Philippines

time : 1 month

comfortable backpacker budget : $1200 | 60,000 Philippine Peso

shoestring budget : $900 | 45,000 Philippine Peso

(budgets don't include the cost of flights to or from The Philippines)

Boracay & Tibiao (1 week)

Boracay is a lively island with wonderful beaches and opportunities to try sailing, wind surfing, snorkelling, diving and jet skiing. It also has a reputation for being a party island although it doesn't get nearly as many westerners as Bali or Thailand for example. Tibiao is about 100km away and has become an eco-adventure destination with river-kayaking along the rapids of the Tibiao River perhaps the highlight. You could maybe do this as a daytrip as there is little accommodation there although it is in the direction of Iloilo City so you could potentially combine it into your journey south.

suggested accommodation: Frendz Resort, near boat station 1, white beach

Iloilo City (1 day)

There's not much here but you'll need to come to Iloilo to get to Cebu and it will break up the journey if you stay overnight.

suggested accommodation: La Fiesta Hotel, M.H. Del Pilar Street

This is a reasonably nice budget hotel but is more costly than most options on this route. There are no real traveller places here.

Cebu (3/4 days)

One of the nicest cities in The Philippines and one of the most important culturally and historically. It has a little bit of everything with excellent museums, markets, nature and warm waters to swim in.

suggested accommodation: G&B Hostel, Jas Building Corner Guadalajara Street, 2nd floor of Mini Stop V. Rama Avenue

Bohol (3/4 days)

The next island down from Cebu Island, it is a tropical region popular with divers and snorkellers and a great place for dolphin and whale watching. The best time of year to come is March to June but it has something to offer year round.

suggested accommodation: Paseo Del Mar Dive Resort, Barangay Pangdan, 6308 Jagna

Dumaguete (1/2 days)

This is a safe and peace-loving city on Negros Island. It's a major university town so there are lots of young people and there are a few decent trips out of town.

suggested accommodation: The Flying Fish Hostel, 32 Hibbard Avenue

Siquijor (3/4 days)

Small island with excellent white sandy beaches, lots of marine life and a mountainous centre perfect for hikes or exploring on a motorbike.

suggested accommodation: Charisma Resort, Solangon, San Juan

Cagayan De Oro (3/4 days)

Reasonably big city but quite a pretty one. The main attraction is white water rafting along the CDO River. In town it's a good place to experience unique Filipino pass-times like Cock-Fighting and Videoke. It should be noted that this is on the large island of Mindanao, which some governments warn their citizens against visiting due to safety concerns.

suggested accommodation: Travelers Pod, G/F Gateway Tower

No real backpacker places so this budget hotel might be your best option although it will be an expensive stay if you are travelling alone.

Camiguin Island (3/4 days)

This is a small island but there's plenty to see and do in different parts of it. There are lots of springs, waterfalls and it is home to no fewer than seven volcanoes.

suggested accommodation: GV Hotel, Burgos Street, Mambajao,

Same story as in Cagayan De Oro.

CONNECTION - Getting from Camiguin Island to Bali, where the Indonesian route begins, is neither simple nor cheap. The most budget-friendly option is likely to be heading back to Manila and then again flying via Kuala Lumpur or Singapore but Philippine Airlines do have direct flights from Manila to Bali. At the time of writing they were an extortionate $280 one-way although you may be able to find better deals by booking in advance.

3.4 PART 4 - Indonesia

time : 1 month

comfortable backpacker budget : $1000 | 13.5 million Indonesian Rupiah

shoestring budget : $750 | 10 million Indonesian Rupiah

(budgets don't include flights to or from Indonesia)

Bali (1 week)

Kuta Beach on Bali has a party scene to rival that of the main Thai Islands and is a great place to spend time meeting other travellers and relaxing on the beach. There is a lot more to Bali than that though and as you explore the island you can learn about the fascinating Hindu Culture, climb mountains and visit sleepy Indonesian fishing villages.

suggested accommodation: The Eco-Living Hostel, Jl. Imam Bonjo, Kuta

Gili Islands (1 week)

These three laid back islands are quieter and much less commercialised rivals to the beaches of Bali but many travellers in Indonesia rate them as their favourite destination. You can easily spend 2 or 3 days on each one or just base yourself on one and visit the others. It's hard to pinpoint what it is, but there is something a little bit special about the Gilis, which are also known for their lack of a police presence and availability of recreational drugs.

suggested accommodation: Gili Castle, Poppies Gang 3, Gili Trawangan

Senggigi Bay (2/3 days)

Senggigi Bay is a pleasant place and you can use it as your base for the epic hike up Mount Rinjani, the second largest volcano in Indonesia. If that sounds a bit too ambitious then there are some great waterfalls which you could head out to instead.

suggested accommodation: Selasar Hostel, Jalan Raya Senggigi No. 9

Kuta Lombok (3 days)

The other side of the island of Lombok is very peaceful and you are now away from the main traveller scene so it's a good spot to relax with some more beach time and reflect as you approach the end of your trip.

suggested accommodation: Same Same Bungalows, Jalan Tebelo

Komodo National Park (3/4 days)

This where you can get close to the Komodo dragons which are one of the iconic images of Indonesia. Diving, kayaking and snorkelling are also options here. Probably best to base yourself in Labuan Bajo where you can sleep safely away from the flesh-eating dragons.

suggested accommodation: Cool Corner Backpacker Hostel, Jl Soekarno Hatta, Labuan Bajo

Kelimutu (2/3 days)

Here you can visit nearby caves, hot springs, giant craters and oddly coloured lakes and learn about many weird local myths relating to them.

suggested accommodation: Antoneri Lodge, Jln. Trans Ende-Maumere, Km 53

Maumere (1 day)

Main airport in this part of Indonesia so it would be a sensible place to end your trip and your best bet would probably be to take a flight to Denpasar or Jakarta and then on from there.

suggested accommodation: Hotel Beng Goan, Jalan Moa Toda 49, Maumere Centre

3.5 Myanmar

time : 3 weeks

comfortable backpacker budget : $650 | 900,000 Burmese Kyat*

shoestring budget : $550 | 750,000 Burmese Kyat*

*Based on official exchange rates. Black market rates may vary considerably.

(doesn't include the cost of transport to Mandalay, the first stop or from Yangon, the end-point.)

This is a separate route to the main one documented in parts 3.1-3.4 but there are various ways to fit it in. Myanmar is most easily accessed from Thailand and flying in and out remains the best option as Myanmar doesn't have that many land crossings with its neighbours and those that do exist are a bit unreliable.

Yangon and Mandalay are the main cities with airports and most travellers start in one and end in the other. You can fly to both from Bangkok with the fare costing around US$40 to Yangon and US$80 to Mandalay. Therefore there are several points on our main route when you can do the trip to Myanmar, starting and ending in Bangkok.

Mandalay (2/3 days)

This is the Second City of Myanmar and although there is not quite as much to do as in Yangon, the city has a famous Royal Palace and is known for its cultural diversity. It is also a major Buddhist centre and is home to half of the country's monks.

suggested accommodation: Yoe Yoe Lay Homestay, between 35-36 street and between 57-58 street

Expect to pay a little bit more for accommodation in Myanmar than in other countries in mainland SE Asia, as decent budget options are limited.

Pyin Oo Lwin (2 days)

The train ride from Pyin Oo Lwin to Hsipaw is the main highlight and is rated as one of the world's most spectacular rail journeys. Pyin Oo Lwin has plenty to offer too though. From the town you can visit some of the local Shan villages and some spectacular waterfalls. The town itself has a weird British vibe with horse and carriages and colonial era houses.

suggested accommodation: Orchid Nan Myaning Hotel, Mandalay-Lasho Road (near Zina Man Aung Kyaut Taung Pagoda)

Hsipaw (2/3 days)

This town has one of the best markets in Myanmar and situated in a valley has some nice hiking opportunities. It is another long journey from Hsipaw to Inle

Lake but in Myanmar you will soon get used to that!

suggested accommodation: Mr Charles Guesthouse, 105 Auba Street, Myo Le Quater

Inle Lake (3 days)

This is another essential stop on almost every backpacking route in Myanmar. It's quite touristy by Burmese standards here but is one of the four main travel highlights in the country (along with Yangon, Mandalay and Bagan). It's a 20km long shallow lake and is home to many different tribes who live on the lake itself so it is a uniquely fascinating place. You can take a day tour of it by boat although it's advisable to try and speak with other travellers before booking one because some are major tourist traps where you are taken to a range of workshops/shops and repetitively encouraged to buy things.

suggested accommodation: Song of Travel Hostel, Aung Chan Thar Street 5, Nandawun Block 6, 11221 Nyaung Shwe

Most of the accommodation is in the village of Nyaung Shwe, just north of the lake. Song of Travel Hostel is very modern and has received rave reviews.

Bagan (3/4 days)

Perhaps the most iconic image of Myanmar. It has the largest and most extensive collection of Buddhist temples, pagodas and ruins in the world and is a truly incredible sight. As well as visiting the temples, you can witness monk and monkess initiation ceremonies and hire a boat out and explore the river. You can also do a daytrip to nearby Mount Popa, which is an extinct volcano but very green and a bit cooler than the hot plains that occupy much of the country.

suggested accommodation: Bagan Central Hotel (Dormitory Rooms), No.15/16, KhaYay Road, New Bagan

Pyay (1/2 days)

It's possible to take a night train all the way to Yangon from Bagan, but it's a long trip so you may wish to break it up by stopping in Pyay, a small town on the

Ayeyarwady River halfway between the two. There's not a great deal to see but that in a way is part of its appeal given the few parts of Myanmar that have opened up to tourism have done so in quite a big way. There's little chance of you falling into tourist traps here because there aren't any. This is a nice spot to grab a bike or hike and explore a rarely visited part of the country.

suggested accommodation: Myat Lodging House, Where Market Street meets Swe Nwe Pagoda Street.

Only a handful of places accept foreigners in Pyay and none are much good. Myat Lodging House will do for a day or two and is conveniently only a 5 minute walk from the train station but you won't be sad to leave.

Yangon (3/4 days)

Yangon is the largest city in Myanmar and main economic centre although it is no longer the capital. British, Chinese and Indian influences are all clearly evident in a city with an intriguing history. It is the perfect place to finish your trip in Myanmar with lots of wonderful pagodas and religious sites as well as the home of Aung San Suu Kyi, whose NLD party won a stunning victory in the 2015 elections in the country.

suggested accommodation: 20th Street Hostel, No. 23, 20 Street Lower Block, Downtown Yangon

There is much more budget accommodation in Yangon than in the rest of the country and competition has helped boost the quality and lower the prices. 20th Street Hostel is a decent bet with cheap dorms by Burmese standards.

3.6 The Best of the Rest

Our routes still miss out large chunks of the region and you'd probably need the best part of a year to visit all the countries for long enough to get a proper feel for them.

There are many Indonesian and Filipino islands that aren't featured that would represent a real adventure. You could easily spend months in either country such is their size and given the sheer number of unique islands they boast. The route only features the most popular destinations in Cambodia and Laos but there are plenty of more remote places in both countries that are worth a visit if you fall in love with either country.

Another option would be to head south after the Thai islands and into Malaysia and finally Singapore rather than heading back North to Bangkok. From Singapore you are very well connected to continue your trip with any of the other three parts of the route although nature lovers will be tempted to instead head over to nearby Borneo and go for a real adventure into the wild.

4) Visas & Border Crossings

4.1 Entry Requirements

The entry requirements for any country are dependent on your nationality. In this section we will indicate the entry requirements for citizens of USA, Canada, Australia, UK, Germany, Ireland and The Netherlands. If you are from Scandinavia, Switzerland and most other EU countries then it is likely you will have the same requirements as Germany and The Netherlands.

If you're from another country, you can also use our visa check tool (www.myfunkytravel.com/visa-check-tool.html) to find out which countries you will need a visa for.

Thailand

No visa is required for all of the nationalities listed above for stays of up to 30 days. Officially you need proof of funds and/or proof of onward travel although in reality this is barely ever asked for. If you want to stay more than 30 days in one stint you will need to apply for a visa before heading to Thailand. Although many travellers, who wish to spend more than 30 days in Thailand simply leave and come back as once you exit Thailand, you can re-enter at any point and get another fresh 30 days for free. If you follow our backpacking route, you will leave Thailand after about 4 weeks and then re-enter later on in your trip so no visa will be required.

If you overstay your visa (or your 30 day visa-free period) you will be charged 500 Baht/day and will get a black mark in your passport. In theory you can also be arrested but this is highly unlikely although given the state of Thai prisons, it's not really worth the risk. There is also the option of extending your stay whilst in Thailand by visiting a local immigration office and purchasing an extension.

Cambodia

30 day visas are available on arrival at all land borders and at the international

airports and must be paid in cash in US Dollars so be sure you have some before you head to Cambodia. All the above nationalities and most other nationals (apart from those from other Southeast Asian countries) must now pay US$30 for a visa following a US$10 increase in October 2014. Small overcharging is common either by the bus companies who offer to sort it for you or by corrupt border officials. It is also possible to get an e-visa online but it is more expensive and not really necessary.

Laos

30 day visas are available on arrival at all the main land borders and at Luang Prabang Airport, Pakse Airport and Wattay Airport in Vientiane. All the above nationalities and most other nationals (apart from Southeast Asian locals) must pay about US$35 for a visa with small variations depending on which country you are from. Again make sure you have sufficient US Dollars before heading to the border as although there are ATMs at most, they typically only dispense Laotian Kip and although you can pay in Kip, it will work out more expensive to do so.

Vietnam

Citizens of Germany and Great Britain can now get 15 days in Vietnam without a visa. At the time of writing all the other nationalities listed above require them. This can be arranged in advance through a Vietnamese embassy or online and typically costs US$20 for stays of 30 days, although multiple companies offer the service so there may be some variation. Rules do regularly change though with plans in place to make e-visas the way of things for everyone so check the latest regulations at the time of travel. Citizens of Sweden, Norway, Finland, Denmark, Japan and South Korea also don't need a visa for stays of up to 15 days. All westerners looking to spend more than 15 days in Vietnam will need to apply for a visa.

Myanmar

Almost all foreigners require a visa including all of the nationalities listed above. 28 day tourist visas can be obtained for US$50 online or at any Myanmar embassy. It's easiest to do this in Bangkok where they offer a same day service and your trip must take place within 3 months of its issue.

You can also get a visa online here - http://evisa.moip.gov.mm

Malaysia

No visa is required for all of the nationalities listed above. Typically you will be issued 30 or 60 days on arrival which can be extended up to 3 months for free if required. Israelis may have difficulty gaining a visa.

Singapore

No visa is required for all of the nationalities listed above. Citizens of 80% of the countries in the world can visit Singapore visa-free for stays of 30-90 days.

The Philippines

No visa is required for all of the nationalities listed above for stays of up to 30 days.

Indonesia

At the time of writing, visas are no longer required for stays of up to 30 days for citizens of any of the countries listed and 169 countries in total. This is provided you enter Indonesia from one of the following main airports or seaports:

Airports: Batam, Surabaya, Medan, Denpasar (Bali), Jakarta (Soekarno-Hatta Airport)

Seaports: Tanjung Uban, Batam, Tanjung Pinang, Tanjung Balai Karimun

This can't be extended though so anyone who wishes to stay more than 30 days will need to sort out a visa in advance with an Indonesian embassy at home or in another country. Alternatively you could do a visa run and leave Indonesia within 30 days before returning.

General Advice for All Countries

To avoid hold-ups and make the border process go smoothly always head to the border with a sufficient amount of US dollars, passport sized photos, a photocopy of your passport and if possible a recent bank statement (showing funds) or future flight confirmations. You probably won't need many of these items but in theory you could be asked. Also make sure the official stamps your passport. You will get in trouble when trying to leave the country if you don't have an entry stamp.

If you want to stay longer than the amount of time listed above then apply for a visa in advance or in some cases it is possible to get a visa extension while you are in the country. This will cost money but won't be as expensive or potentially troublesome as overstaying your welcome.

4.2 Border Crossings

Some of these borders do have a habit of changing their opening hours and even closing for several days or longer depending on the mood of the local authorities. The Burma-Thailand borders are especially renowned for this so it is important you check the current situation before aimlessly heading to the border. Staff in your hostel should know the answer and be sure to allow enough time to get there before it closes.

Often you can buy direct international bus tickets where you get off at the border to go through passport control and hop back on at the other side. This might not be the cheapest option but tends to be the most hassle free one. Many of the border towns are miserable places full of people eager to trick you and rip you off so it's generally best not to hang around long.

At the time of research, these are the official legal international land border crossings in the region that are open to foreigners:

THAILAND & MALAYSIA

Sadao - Changloon

Padang Besar - Kaki Bukir

Betong - Keroh

Sungai Golok - Pasir Mas

THAILAND & LAOS

Chiang Khong - Houei Xai (Bo Keo)

Huay Khon - Muang Ngeun (Hongsa)

Tha Li - Nam Heuang (Kenthao)

Nong Khai - Friendship Bridge (Vientiane)

Beung Kan - Pakxan

Nakhon Phanom - Tha Khek

Mukdahan - Savannakhet

Chong Mek - Vang Tao (Pakse)

THAILAND & CAMBODIA

Aranyaprathet - Poipet

Hat Lek (Klong Yai) - Pak Khlong (Ko Kong)

Kap Cheong - O Smach

Chong Sa Ngam - Anlong Veng

Ban Pagkard - Phsa Prum

Ban Laem - Daun Lem

THAILAND & MYANMAR

Mae Sai - Tachilek

Mae Sot - Myawadi

Ranong - Victoria Point

Phu Nam Ron - Htee Khee

LAOS & VIETNAM

Pang Hok (Muang Khua) - Tay Trang (Mai Chau)

Dene Savan (Savannakhet) - Lao Bao (Khung Tri)

Nam Phao (Bolikhamsai) - Cau Treo (Vinh)

Nam Kanh (Phonsavan) - Nam Can

Nam Soy (Xam Neua) - Na Meo

Phou Keua (Attapeu) - Bo Y (Kon Tum)

LAOS & CAMBODIA

Dong Kralaw (Voeung Kham) - (Dong Crorlor) Stung Treng

VIETNAM & CAMBODIA

Moc Bai - Bavet

Vinh Xuong (Chau Doc) - Khaom Samnor (Phom Den)

SINGAPORE & MALAYSIA

Woodlands - Johore Bahru

Tuas - Tanjong Kupang

MALAYSIA & INDONESIA

Tebedu - Entikong

Lundu-Biawak - Aruk-Sambas

MYANMAR & LAOS

Although there is a land border between the two countries, at the time of writing there is currently no legal point where foreigners can cross so you'll have to go via Thailand or fly. Plans are in place to open a crossing and it may be open at some point in 2017 or 2018 so check for updates.

BORDER CROSSINGS ON OUR ROUTE (3.1 to 3.5)

Look at a map and you can probably work out quickly enough which would be the most logical for your trip. There are a few other unofficial crossings but unless you get lost it's unlikely you will need them! In any case they are not legal places for foreigners to cross though it may still be possible with a small bribe or 'unofficial fee'.

If you follow the route in section 3 then the most sensible border crossings are as follows:

Aranyaprathet (Thailand) - Poipet (Cambodia)

On one side of the border lurks an army of Thai Policeman looking to bust anyone bringing drugs in from often lawless Cambodia (If you're heading the other way, chances are your bus will be stopped and inspected by sniffer dogs). On the other side lies an army of conmen, tricksters and general nuisances. Poipet is the most dislikeable place in Cambodia. Don't let first impressions put you off!

Bavet (Cambodia) - Moc Bai (Vietnam)

Cambodian border-towns are generally peculiar places and this one is no different. The long road approaching the border is lined with large casinos aimed at enticing in the Vietnamese who are not allowed to gamble in their own country. Once on the other side it's not far to Ho Chi Minh City and there is no point in hanging around in Moc Bai. Most travellers do this as a direct bus from Phnom Penh to HCMC so you don't need to worry much but make sure you have sorted your Vietnamese visa in advance, if you need one.

Vietnam - Laos

It is advisable to fly between Vietnam and Laos unless you like long journeys and don't suffer from travel sickness in which case the **Xam Neua - Na Meo** or **Nam Kanh - Nam Can** crossings are the most viable. Consider stopping at a few other destinations between Hanoi and Vientiane if you go down that road.

Houei Xai (Laos) - Chiang Khong (Thailand)

This is actually one of the nicest border crossings in Southeast Asia and the towns on either side have enough going for them to warrant a stay for a day or two which is an extreme rarity in this part of the world.

Thailand - The Philippines

Getting from Thailand to The Philippines is only possible by flying and Bangkok to Manila is the most regular connection, although indirect flights via Singapore or Kuala Lumpur are cheaper.

The Philippines - Indonesia

The same pretty much goes for The Philippines to Indonesia although for those determined to limit flights to the absolute minimum it is theoretically possible to do it without flying although it's not advisable.

In theory you can island hop all the way to one of the southernmost Philippine islands and catch a boat from Zamboanga city (supposedly a dangerous place with some terrorist activity) to Sandakan in Malaysian Borneo. From there you can cross by land into Indonesia however the only official crossings are on the other side of the island in Western Borneo. Given that Borneo is the third largest island in the world, it may take a while. Good luck with that!

Thailand - Myanmar

If you plan on visiting Myanmar, then again flying in and out is likely to be your best option. By land, Mae Sot/Myawaddy is the border crossing with the best links to Myanmar's rather limited transport network. The border is located only one kilometre from Myawaddy bus station on the Myanmar side and five kilometres from the town of Mae Sot in Thailand. There are plenty of moto-taxis on both sides of the border, which will take you to either.

There are regular buses and daily flights to Mae Sot from Chiang Mai and Bangkok. From Myawaddy, it is 150km to Hpa-An, which is well worth visiting before heading on to Bago and Yangon.

5) Budgeting

5.1 Money

Each country has its own money but the US Dollar is the main reserve currency in the region and is used even more regularly than the national currency in some parts of Southeast Asia. In Cambodia and Vietnam it is common to pay in US Dollars for many things and if there is change you might get it in the local currency. If you're planning on taking cash with you to the region, US Dollars would be a wise choice but it also can be withdrawn from cash machines in countries where it is widely used. It's not a good idea to carry thousands of dollars in cash for the duration of your trip and you can usually get reasonable exchange rates at ATM's (as good as or better than the cash exchange places).

If you travel to more remote areas be sure you have enough cash for the trip before you set off as in much of Laos, Cambodia, Myanmar and Indonesia, ATM's are far from plentiful and the ones that do exist are unreliable. While you don't want to be carrying huge wads of cash with you everywhere, if you're heading into more rural areas (even in the more developed countries) then don't rely on the fact that there will be a functioning cash machine.

The national currencies are as follows:

Thailand - baht (THB)

Cambodia - riel (KHR)

Laos - kip (pronounced keep) (LAK)

Vietnam - dong (VND)

Myanmar - Burmese kyat (MMK)

Malaysia - ringgit (RM)

Singapore - Singapore dollar (S$)

The Philippines - peso (PHP)

Indonesia - rupiah (IDR)

As of February 2017, these are the current exchange rates:

1 US DOLLAR is worth:

THB - 35.01

KHR - 4058

LAK - 8220

VND - 22619

MMK* - 1359

RM - 4.42

S$ - 1.41

PHP - 49.59

IDR – 13296

1 EURO is worth:

THB - 37.49

KHR - 4345

LAK - 8805

VND - 24198

MMK* - 1457

RM - 4.74

S$ - 1.51

PHP - 53.13

IDR - 14248

US$ - 1.07

1 BRITISH POUND is worth:

THB - 43.59

KHR - 5051

LAK - 10232

VND - 28123

MMK* - 1693

RM - 5.51

S$ - 1.75

PHP - 61.76

IDR - 16556

US$ - 1.25

* The exchange rate for Myanmar is the official one. You can get a much better deal on the black market.

If your currency isn't featured here then research this before you go and it is a good idea to make a note of the exchange rates for all the currencies in the region as well as the US Dollar. It's especially useful when entering new countries at border crossings as those places are full of guys offering currency exchange at awful rates and looking to make a quick buck off naive newcomers.

You can check current rates and the exchange rates for other currencies on

5.2 Typical Backpacking Costs in Southeast Asia

People come to Southeast Asia with greatly varying budgets and there is a lot of conflicting information out there about what a realistic budget might be. As a result we have a suggested shoestring and more comfortable backpacker budget for each country in this section.

Possible Daily Shoestring Budget (in US Dollars)

The following is designed to be a rough guide and is based on staying in budget hostels, eating in local restaurants or street stalls and travelling by local buses, trains or boats as opposed to more expensive tourist options. It gives you room for a bit of partying and a few extra activities like jungle treks, rafting expeditions and suchlike but if you are doing things like that every day and drinking most nights you will spend more!

In other words, the budget requires some discipline. It also doesn't allow for major expenses like scuba-diving courses or multi-day organised tours. It does not include flights to or from the region nor does it include pre-trip expenses on things like vaccinations and travel insurance which can be quite costly. The same applies for the budgets quoted in the routes chapter.

$20/day : Cambodia, Laos, Vietnam

$25/day : Malaysia*, Indonesia, Thailand, Myanmar

$30/day : The Philippines

$45/day : Singapore

*This is based on costs on Peninsular Malaysia (mainland). Borneo is much more expensive to travel in.

If you are not a party animal and aren't planning many extra activities then it is possible to get by on less than this. In big countries like Indonesia and Malaysia, costs vary greatly between the regions. For example in Indonesia the cost of travelling in parts of Java and Bali is probably double what it would be in say Sumatra. Therefore the figures should at least be a useful guideline but are by no means an exact science. If you try to cram in a lot and visit many different places rather than spending longer in fewer destinations this will also push your costs up.

As a guideline most travellers in Southeast Asia end up spending more than the figures quoted but they are by no means unrealistic for genuine shoestring travellers.

Possible Shoestring Budget for whole Trip in SE Asia

1 month - £650, €750, $800

2 months - £1300, €1500, $1600

3 months - £1950, €2250, $2400

4 months - £2600, €3000, $3200

5 months - £3250, €3750, $4000

6 months - £3900, €4500, $4800

In addition to this you may want to allow for perhaps another £1000 (roughly $1250) for a return flight to the region, travel insurance and vaccinations. Obviously this figure depends hugely on where you live and what kind of deals you can get on those things.

If you stay just in mainland Southeast Asia, it may be that you can get by on less than this budget. If you want to visit all the countries then it will be more as you will have to fork out for a lot more connecting flights.

Some budget travellers have managed to explore mainland Southeast Asia in 4 months for as little as $1500. Others who get sucked into the party culture or prefer to splash out a little more for better quality accommodation easily manage to spend double these figures. If it's your first backpacking trip it would be wise to factor in a little more than this as it's not always immediately obvious how to find the best budget options and you are likely to make the odd expensive mistake.

More Comfortable Daily Backpacking Budget

The following is what could be classed as a more typical budget these days, primarily because of the partying element of backpacking in Southeast Asia, which will take up a sizable chunk of your daily spend if you're a big drinker or party animal. Temptation is always around the corner here, even in the day-time with extra trips and excursions possible at almost every stop on the Southeast Asian backpacking trail.

$25/day : Cambodia, Vietnam

$30/day : Laos, Malaysia*, Myanmar

$35/day : Indonesia

$40/day : Thailand, Philippines

$70/day : Singapore

*This is based on costs on Peninsular Malaysia (mainland). Borneo is much more expensive to travel in.

Note that Thailand in particular sees a big jump from the 'shoestring budget'. This is down to a combination of the party culture and wide array of extra activities that are on offer here. Singapore is similar with restaurants and bars very expensive even by Western standards and plenty of options for spending cash. On the other hand, somewhere like Myanmar doesn't have as much of either so there is less danger of you going massively over-budget.

In the larger countries like Indonesia, how much you spend will depend on how much travelling around you do. Cramming a lot into a short space of time, then this budget may not even cover it. Sticking on one of the cheaper islands and travelling at a less frenetic pace, you could probably get by on less than even the shoestring budget.

More Comfortable Monthly Backpacking Budget in Southeast Asia

1 month - £800, €925, $1000

2 months - £1600, €1850, $2000

3 months - £2400, €2775, $3000

4 months - £3200, €3700, $4000

5 months - £4000, €4625, $5000

6 months - £4800, €5500, $6000

$1000/month is a decent benchmark figure to look at when planning your trip. Even if you have some experience of travelling on a budget, you'd be wise to allow for this but frugal backpackers should be able to get by on less.

The exchange rates to Euros and Pounds in this chapter are based on February 2017 rates. They changed drastically in 2016 alone so keep an eye out for any major alterations as it could make your trip considerably cheaper or more expensive.

6) Best Festivals

Southeast Asia is home to some weird and wonderful festivals. For a truly memorable experience try and fit at least one of these into your trip. Remember to book beds and transport in advance during festival time as budget options will sell out quickly.

1st January 2017, 1st January 2018

Aguman Sanduk

Manila, the Philippines

The Philippines has some of the best and certainly most colourful festivals in Asia and its capital welcomes in every New Year in a most unique fashion. Over 80 years ago on New Year's Day a group of blokes in a moment of drunken inspiration thought it would be nice to dress up in women's clothing and wander around the streets as a way of welcoming in the New Year. The idea proved a hit and from that point it grew with each passing year into a giant parade of bra wearing, handbag wielding men. The tradition remains very much alive and many respectable gentleman discover their secret feminine side every New Year's Day.

20th-22nd January 2017, Dates TBC for 2018

Dinagyang

Iloilo City, the Philippines

This festival is actually the younger sibling of Ati-Atihan which celebrates the same thing in nearby Kalibo (it's easy enough to visit both) but in many ways this one is more fun and foreigners are very much welcomed and able to take part. Although it has religious and cultural origins, the festival is predominantly about extravagant costumes and carefree dancing. It is not dissimilar to the Rio Carnival on a much smaller yet more accessible scale. The main event is the Ati Ati Grand Parade, which is a competition between various local tribes who attempt to outshine each other. After the results, things turn into an exuberant street party. All in all it's great fun!

9th February 2017, 31st January 2018

Thaipusam

Kuala Lumpur, Malaysia

KL is a very multicultural city and it celebrates many religious festivals but the Hindu Festival of Thaipusam is certainly the most intriguing. The day starts at the Sri Mahamariamman Temple at noon and ends after dusk in the spooky Batu Caves across the city with hundreds of thousands making the 15km pilgrimage across town. Participants perform incredible acts of devotion to show their penance to the Hindu God Lord Murugan. Some pierce large portions of their body while others carry or drag heavy metal objects all the way up to the shrine at the top of the caves. You might prefer to join the many who just come along for the ride.

28th January 2017, 16th February 2018

Chinese New Year

All over Southeast Asia. Probably best in Hanoi.

There is a large Chinese influence on Southeast Asian culture and most of the big cities have sizeable Chinese communities that hold lavish Chinese New Year festivities. Events take place over the course of a fortnight with giant feasts, firework displays and dragon parades taking place. Northern Vietnam has the closest links to China and Hanoi is an excellent place to take in the Chinese New Year. Apart from the spectacle, there are many important traditional rituals that families go through to prepare for the New Year which are worth finding out about.

14th-17th April 2017, 30th March - 2nd April 2018

Easter

San Fernando, the Philippines

In much of the Christian world people spend Easter lazing around eating chocolate and painting eggs. In The Philippines on Easter Sunday people crucify themselves. Each year about two dozen locals in the town of San Fernando and a few other towns around the country volunteer themselves to be nailed to a cross in recognition of Jesus' sacrifice and resurrection. While these clearly mortal folks are brought down after 20 minutes or so into the arms of waiting medics, the nails, blood and pain is all very real.

Good news folks, this is another festival where travellers can take part. In 2014 a young Danish man joined twenty odd Filipinos in getting himself 'crucified'. The Vatican is said to frown upon these annual rituals but Lasse Spang Olsen described it as 'a great experience'. Each to their own.

13th-15th April 2017, 13th-15th April 2018

Songkran

Thailand - best in Bangkok or Chiang Mai

What better way to celebrate the Buddhist New Year than getting a super-soaker out and drenching people with cold water. This is basically just a giant water fight. It is supposed to symbolise spiritual cleansing and given that it takes place at the hottest time of year it does come as a welcome relief from the heat. The festival is a terrific spectacle, especially in the big cities and is a whole load of fun. If you're clearly foreign you're even more of a target so prepare to get very wet!

May - June 2017, May - June 2018 (exact dates vary between towns)

Boun Bang Fai Rocket Festival

Laos - perhaps best in Luang Prabang

It's worth heading to Laos for this extravaganza not least because there is something childishly wonderful about saying 'Boun Bang Fai Rocket'. It is held in towns and villages all over Laos at the beginning of the rainy season to pray for rain and a good harvest. It involves people building and firing rockets as high into the sky as they can manage (quite what this has to do with praying for rain is not entirely clear). The winners get whisky while those whose rockets prove to be massive flops get greeted with jeers and laughter.

14th July - 16th July 2017, Dates TBC for 2018

Rainforest World Music Festival

Kuching, Malaysia

One of the best music festivals in the region. 35 miles outside the town of Kuching, through vast swamps of jungle you reach the base of Mount Santubong where thousands of music enthusiasts from all over the world gather for this three day affair. It is as the name suggests a celebration of world music so you can expect a large variety of genres and nationalities to be represented. The vibe is extremely friendly with many tiny sets in the afternoon where you can get up close and personal with the artists before the larger evening performances on the two main stages.

www.rwmf.net

20th-28th October 2017, Dates TBC for 2018

Phuket Vegetarian Festival

Phuket, Thailand

This might not sound like it's going to be a whole barrel of joy and fun but in fact it is completely insane! There are more worryingly sadistic thrills to be had here with gruesome acts of self-torture taking place in an attempt to rid the body of evil spirits. It is nearly two hundred years old now and each year it continues to get more shocking. Bring your camera and take some of the most unusual snaps of your life!

3rd-5th November 2017, Dates TBC for 2018

Yi Peng & Loy Krathong (Lantern Festival)

Chiang Mai, Thailand

This is one for those who want a slice of traditional Southeast Asian pie. Loy

Krathong is an enchanting spectacle that takes place every year to coincide with the full moon in November. Thousands of small lanterns are released into the air and quickly illuminate the night sky while rivers and lakes are filled with mini boats made out of banana leaves. It's a Buddhist tradition and it symbolises the removal of worries and release of suffering as the year draws to a close.

7) Where to Party

7.1 Top 10 Party Destinations

1. Koh Phangan, Thailand

This island has achieved legendary status in backpacking folklore ever since a few hippies held the first full moon parties decades ago on Haad Rin beach. Phangan doesn't just party once a month however and no matter when you arrive there will be some lively all night affair going on for you to get your teeth into. While it has become more commercialised over the years, the lack of an airport has kept package tourists away and it still retains much of the magic that travellers fell in love with in the 1980s and 1990s. There is more on the beach parties in the next section.

2. Kuta Beach (Bali), Indonesia

Bali has long been a popular nightlife destination for Aussies and with great surf and jumping nightlife it's easy to see why. Kuta is Indonesia's only major party resort town and one of the few places that can rival Thailand in this part of the world for its intense traveller party crowd. With nightly events of various themes and wonderfully named strong cocktails, Kuta is great fun and has an excellent beach for recovering on the next day.

3. Sihanoukville, Cambodia

Cambodia's best nightlife option, Sihanoukville is home to some of the wildest nights in Southeast Asia and whatever hour of day it is, chances are someone, somewhere will be partying. Its beaches are beautiful, the drinks are cheap and the alcohol flows 24-7. Certainly a bit of a drug culture has built up here too and it is the sort of the place where you can lose control of yourself if you're not careful.

4. Koh Phi Phi, Thailand

Phi Phi was a sleepy, peaceful island paradise before a young Leonardo Dicaprio rocked up at the turn of the millennium in the movie 'The Beach'. Since then it has rapidly built up into a travel hotspot and Phi Phi Don has turned into another raucous party island. It has recovered well since the devastating tsunami a decade ago and as far as partying in paradise goes this takes some beating. There are all sorts of mental drinking games to get involved with and plenty of inventive ways to earn yourself a free bucket from stripping butt naked to jumping in the muay thai boxing ring and fighting another foolhardy amateur.

5. Boracay, the Philippines

This is where Filipinos come to let their hair down and outsiders are starting to wake up to beautiful Boracay too. It' a small island well away from the busy cities with perfect beaches. Bars that hug the beachside serve up cheap drinks and plenty of fun till dawn. Whether you want chilled out local affairs, excellent live music or sweaty dancefloors Boracay doesn't disappoint.

6. Bangkok, Thailand

A true city of sin and temptation, Bangkok is not everyone's cup of tea but its unique brand of nightlife is eye-opening if nothing else. The go-go bars are easy enough to avoid and even once you're getting sick of the Khao San Road and its bustling traveller bars, there is a whole city to explore with a wide range of nightlife options from budget street parties to luxurious mega-clubs. Whatever floats your boat, you can bet on finding it somewhere in Bangkok.

7. Gili Trawangan, Indonesia

The lack of a police presence on the island leads to one thing. Mayhem. Drugs are available on the menu in many bars and restaurants and generally there are three big party nights each week when everyone goes mental. The rest of the time it's fairly sedate and quiet with people recovering and gearing up for the next party on Gili T. Although there are no permanent police stationed on the island, occasionally there are surprise raids and Indonesian drug laws and punishments are extremely tough.

8. Jakarta, Indonesia

The capital of the world's largest Islamic state might seem like an unlikely party destination but if you know where to find it, Jakarta has some totally insane nightlife. It has giant clubs that open on Friday night and don't shut until Monday morning and many revellers party for days or more (with a little extra help from certain narcotics). For those who like their nightlife a little bit 'rough around the edges' then this monstrous city might just be for you.

9. Singapore

Expensive it may be but Singapore does have some of the best nightclubs in Asia and weekends are very lively. You might struggle to get in to many places if you turn up in your scruffy beach clothes so be sure to dress up in something reasonably smart. There are a few bars and clubs with 24 hour licences and many places are open past 3am. Friday and Saturday are the biggest nights while girls get in free and get free drinks on ladies night which is Wednesday or Thursday in most places. Sunday is gay night in many clubs. If you want to do it local style then hit the nearest K-Box with some friends for a night of karaoke. Bring your wallet though as alcohol is very expensive.

10. Ho Chi Minh City, Vietnam

Old Saigon was where American soldiers let their hair down during the Vietnam War and today there is a new brand of westerners that are enjoying the nightlife of the city. There are plenty of places worth avoiding and many bars are brimming with local prostitutes and sleazy old white men but amongst the mess there are some gems. The Pham Ngu Lao area has some lively bars and clubs that party well past midnight and it is home to the country's best backpacker orientated nightlife.

7.2 Full Moon Parties

Once a month, travellers in Southeast Asia converge on the Thai island of Koh Phangan for a night of revelling and debauchery. The length of Haad Rin Beach is taken over by alcohol stalls, sound-systems, pumping beats and painted bodies. It's trashy but unashamedly good fun and for many one of the defining moments of a trip to Southeast Asia.

As has been mentioned previously it is a good idea to arrive well in advance of Full Moon night itself to both secure accommodation and enjoy what Koh Phangan has to offer at your leisure. The run up to the main event includes jungle and pool parties which are well organised affairs and often equally wild. Although you may prefer to spend your time chilling on the beach and exploring the iconic mushroom mountain which is home to a few bars that continue to serve magic mushroom shakes. Whatever you do make sure you are feeling fresh for full moon as it's not the sort of party you leave early.

Expected Full Moon Party nights for 2017 & 2018 are as follows:

Thursday 12th January 2017

Sunday 12th February 2017

Sunday 12th March 2017

Tuesday 11th April 2017

Thursday 11th May 2017

Friday 9th June 2017

Monday 10th July 2017

Monday 7th August 2017

Tuesday 5th September 2017

Friday 6th October 2017

Friday 3rd November 2017

Sunday 3rd December 2017

Monday 1st January 2018

Wednesday 31st January 2018

Friday 2nd March 2018

Saturday 31st March 2018

Monday 30th April 2018

Tuesday 29th May 2018

Thursday 28th June 2018

Friday 27th July 2018

Sunday 26th August 2018

Tuesday 25th September 2018

Wednesday 24th October 2018

Friday 23rd November 2018

Saturday 22nd December 2018

Occasionally there are changes and the parties may not fall exactly on full moon night but it'll only be a day or two either side.

Full moon party dates are updated here - www.phangan.info/index.cfm?action=night.dates

In addition, the biggest parties with the most people take place on New Year's Eve even though they don't necessarily coincide with a full moon. The 2017 NYE party does fall very close to a full moon though so it should be an epic affair.

They also hold Christmas parties if you want the maddest but probably least festive Christmas Day of your life. The festive period is considered peak season in Thailand as the weather is great and hundreds of thousands flock to the country from around the world but as you would expect prices rise and accommodation quickly sells out.

Christmas & New Year Parties:

25th December 2017: Christmas Party

31st December 2017: New Year Party

1st January 2018: New Year After Party

25th December 2018: Christmas Party

31st December 2018: New Year Party

Every week throughout the year when there isn't a Full Moon party there will be either a half-moon or black-moon party. These are slightly smaller events with a different vibe but tend to attract a friendlier crowd. Both are predominantly trance affairs and have a more underground feel. The black moon parties take place once a month on Baan Tai beach while the Half Moon Festival takes place about a week before and a week after Full Moon in the jungle with regular truck shuttles provided from Haad Rin Beach. Exact dates aren't announced as far in advance.

8) Top 10 Places to Experience Local Culture

There is a huge variety of different cultures to be found within the region. While at times you have to differentiate what's real from what's just for show to bring in fat tourist dollars you shouldn't have too much trouble discovering authentic local traditions and customs.

Here are ten of the best places to do it:

Bagan, Myanmar

On the banks of the Ayeyarwady River in Central Myanmar lies the truly extraordinary area of Bagan. It is home to the largest collection of Buddhist pagodas, temples and ruins anywhere in the world. Some of the structures are almost 1000 years. Although few are as impressive as those at Angkor, the sheer number is what is remarkable. The town itself is a fairly laid back place. If you're an early riser you might just catch some of the rituals that the monks and monkettes (yes there are female monks) go through each morning or even a novice monk initiation ceremony.

Bali, Indonesia

For many outsiders Bali is just a beach with a few bars and lots of Australians. In reality it is an island with a thriving and proud Hindu culture, unique in the predominantly Islamic Indonesia. The island is small enough to explore in a few days but big enough that there is a large variety of ways to experience Balinese culture. Your time can be spent at bustling local markets, arts and crafts shops, temples and museums which are found all over the island from scenic mountain towns to picturesque fishing villages.

Chiang Mai, Thailand

If Bangkok, is Thailand's economic and political heart, then Chiang Mai is certainly the cultural one. It is the home of a host of ancient Thai practices and given that it's a big backpacker hotspot, it's very easy for you to observe or even take part in them. Some experiences are more authentic than others but this is the sort of town you could hang around for weeks, spend very little yet learn a great deal about Thai cooking, Thai massage (the traditional version) and traditional Buddhist practices such as meditation. There are also lots of interesting ethnic groups and tribes in the area and for once Thailand might just leave you enlightened and uplifted as opposed to hungover and sunburnt.

Tana Toraja, Indonesia (Sulawesi Island)

The island of Sulawesi doesn't get many visitors with most travellers in Indonesia opting for Java, Bali or Lombok. Those who do come will be richly rewarded with rock bottom prices and fascinating local traditions. Tana Toraja translates to 'The Land of Heavenly Kings' and its inhabitants are a predominantly Christian ethnic group known as the Torajans.

Of their many rituals it is the spectacular death ceremonies that really stand out. The funeral is treated as the most important ceremony in the life of a Torajan as it is believed they continue to look over and protect their families after death. As such it can take many months of planning and involves the purchases of buffalos and pigs which are sacrificed at the main event. The funeral season takes place during July and August but it's a fascinating destination year round and Rantepao, the cultural centre is a good starting point.

Angkor Wat, Cambodia

While the nearby settlement of Siem Reap, where you will probably stay is little more than a tourist trap with little authentic local culture, Angkor Wat is Cambodia's pride and joy. It is the symbol of the nation, it's on the flag and it is what people here are most proud of. The sad reality is that Cambodia peaked close to 1000 years ago and after a century of destruction inflicted from within as well as from outside there's not a great deal left worth bragging about. To understand Khmer culture and the national psyche you have to look back to the glorious past which is remarkably well preserved by the dense jungle that engulfs the Temples of Angkor Wat.

Luang Prabang, Laos

This is perhaps the cultural highlight of Laos. There is something enchanting and uniquely Southeast Asian about the goings on in Luang Prabang. Young monks dressed head to toe in orange robes roam the elegant streets which point to secrets from the town's mix of French and Indochinese heritage. With temples and museums galore it's easy enough to scratch beneath surface and discover the journey that Luang Prabang has been through.

Hoi An, Vietnam

Hoi An is a really special place nestled in the heart of Vietnam. Its idyllic riverside location and cobblestone streets ooze history and Vietnamese tradition and for a few split seconds you'd be forgiven for thinking you had stepped back into the 14th or 15th century. Old fashioned boats line the riverbanks and ignoring the odd very decent rock bar (geared towards the increasing influx of travellers) you sense many people's lives haven't changed that much from that of their ancestors. The town's speciality is tailor-made clothes and you may well end up leaving here with more items in your backpack than you arrived with.

Georgetown (Penang), Malaysia

Malaysia is home to a big mix of nationalities, cultures and customs and its open acceptance of each is perhaps the country's most striking quality. Nowhere is this more evident than Georgetown on Penang Island where its colonial British style streets and buildings are home to many small communities from different parts of Asia with Little India and Chinatown the largest. Everything is within walking distance and there's enough exotic variety of food to last you for weeks sampling different world cuisines. Once referred to as the 'Pearl of the Orient' in colonial times, Georgetown still holds a special charm.

Yogyakarta, Indonesia (Java Island)

Known as Jogja to locals and a small but steady flow of backpackers that fill up the budget accommodation in alleyways close to the town's main train station. The town itself has always had a reputation for attracting arts dealers from across Asia and is home to many impressive galleries and several significant palaces and monuments that show off different aspects of Islamic and Javanese culture and history.

It is also very close to two of Indonesia's most important and impressive religious sites. Firstly the magnificent Borobudur, the world's largest Buddhist monument outshines even Angkor Wat in terms of its size and grandeur. At sunrise especially it is a truly awe-inspiring sight. The other one is the Hindu temples at Prambanan which are equally important and it is easy to visit both Borobudur and Prambanan on the same day although prepare for some fairly hefty entry fees of around US$20 at each site.

Inle Lake, Myanmar

This is a special place deep in the heart of Burma. The lake is 22km long but its waters are only very shallow and many thousands of people live on the lake itself which is shared by various different tribes. Some of the tours of the lake are lacking in real authenticity as the stops are at purpose built workshops which put on shows for tourists so talk to other travellers and try to get a recommendation. On dry land cultural highlights include Aung's Marionette Puppet Show featuring traditional Burmese music in a local theatre.

9) Best Destinations for Adventure & Nature

9.1 Five Activities for Active Travellers & Adrenaline Junkies

While the parties are fun, they probably aren't the things you will remember in 10 or 20 year's time (or even the next morning) and lets face it you can party anywhere. Can you climb up a giant lava-spewing volcano or hurtle down furious rapids where you come from? Whether you're from Barnsley or Basel, Munich or Maine, the answer is probably not.

Southeast Asia serves up a fair dose of adventure and gives visitors the chance to do things that they might never get the opportunity to do again. It would be foolish not to take advantage of that especially given that the prices are on the whole very cheap. Here are 5 of the best activities:

Scuba Diving in Koh Tao, Thailand

The isolated Thai island of Koh Tao is a fantastic place to explore the depths of the ocean. It's perfect for people with no experience as in a week you can pick up a qualification and the knowledge which will allow you to go diving anywhere in the future. The course includes some classroom time and practice in a pool before you head out to explore the island's marine life. Backpacking trips are great fun but it's also nice to go home feeling as though you have achieved something and picked up a new skill along the way. The courses typically include accommodation and can be arranged in advance or on the island.

White-water Rafting & Kayaking in Cagayan de Oro, Philippines

The Philippines is an excellent destination for adventure travellers and those who like to do lots of active things. One of the best places is Cagayan de Oro (CDO). The rapids along the CDO River are perfect for white-water rafting. They are at their wildest during the rainy season in September and October but novices might be advised to head here at any other time of year. If that's not enough, managing the rapids on your own in a kayak is even greater fun although quite challenging.

Skydiving at the Lido Lakes, Indonesia

Less than a couple of hours outside the urban monstrosity that is Jakarta, you reach the Lido Lakes which couldn't be any more different from the Indonesian capital if they tried. With huge gaping valleys and a couple of ominous looking volcanoes, it is an incredible setting for a skydive. Whether you're a beginner seeking your first dive or you have lots of previous experience this is just about the best place in Southeast Asia for the sport. Once back on safe ground you can explore the beautiful surroundings on horseback.

Kitesurfing in Mui Ne, Vietnam

The gorgeous beach of Mui Ne in Vietnam is an idyllic place to relax and its waters and winds serve up perfect kitesurfing conditions. The bay is so big that things never get overcrowded and with barely any rainfall and consistent surf, it is usually a picturesque view of kite and windsurfers sharing the sea with Vietnamese fishing boats. Overall it's a fantastic budget friendly destination to learn and practice one of the most enjoyable watersports.

Rock Climbing at Railay Beach, Thailand

You might have experienced rock climbing at a small indoor centre in a local town but this is totally incomparable. There are no long safety videos or demonstrations and you can even go totally rope and gear free on the cliffs of Railay in Southern Thailand with the blue warm water of the Andaman Sea acting as your safety net. It is known as Deep Water Soloing and although it can be a challenging activity, there are routes of varying difficulty and all you need to do is turn up and give it a go. The bay is surrounded by large cliffs and more traditional rock-climbing and a range of other activities can also be done.

9.2 Five Natural Wonders

Halong Bay, Vietnam

Halong Bay is the most beautiful place in Vietnam and a true natural wonder which hasn't yet been spoiled by mass tourism although numbers are certainly on the up. It's best explored on a boat trip around the area which will take up at least a full day if you want to see the best of it. You can explore caves, swim in tiny creaks and enjoy the sun setting over these stunning limestone islets.

Borneo, Indonesia & Malaysia

The mere mention of the word Borneo conjures up images of jungles, lagoons, wild creatures and tropical adventures. It's bigger than the vast majority of the countries in the world but even the Malaysian part in the North is almost entirely rural and cut off from modern civilisation. Most of the island belongs to Indonesia and much of it is so remote that it scarcely receives any visitors and sections are almost entirely inaccessible. If you're looking for adventure, lengthy jungle treks and plenty of surprises then you could easily spend weeks or months exploring Borneo alone but it's probably not the best place to start if you don't have much experience of independent travel.

Hpa-An, Myanmar

A small and fairly average town in Southeastern Myanmar but it is a base for exploring some of the fantastic surrounding areas. There are lots of curious caves to discover with the giant Saddar cave and its reclining Buddha and the Bat Cave the best ones. The latter is best visited at sunset when a ridiculous number of bats (hundreds of thousands) fly out of it only to return the following morning. You can also rent a bike or motorbike and explore the tranquil Burmese countryside. Another option is to climb all the way to the top of Mount Zwegabin which is home to a monastery where the resident monks will let you sleep.

Komodo National Park, Indonesia

As far as Southeast Asia's most remarkable creature goes, it surely has to be the mythical Komodo dragon. The Komodo national Park consists of a trio of small islands just west of the larger island of Flores in Indonesia. The menacing looking multi-talented dragons are surprisingly fast movers over land, capable swimmers and possess the ability to jump to a fairly serious height. They occasionally have a taste for human flesh so it is extremely advisable to seek a guide who will show you around for about 70,000Rp.

The park is also home to wild horses, boar, deer, water buffalos, monkeys, snakes (of the poisonous variety) while its waters are inhabited by whales, dolphins and various other forms of marine life. It's an effort to get here but lovers of all things wildlife will not regret it and almost certainly will never forget it.

Bohol, Philippines

This Filipino island is a real natural paradise and ticks all the boxes when it comes to nature and adventure. The shores of the island are awash with gentle rolling white beaches, marine life and little coves. It's home to whales, dolphins and the Tarsier, said to be the world's smallest primate. Bohol is surrounded by 75 little islets, many of which are uninhabited although only a short boat ride away. If you're lucky you might just get to spend a day on your own private island!

10) First Timers in Southeast Asia – FAQs

Do I need to book accommodation in advance?

Generally speaking the answer to this is no as there is no shortage of budget accommodation in most of Southeast Asia. Exceptions are for big festivals and certainly for the days around big events like the full moon party on Koh Phangan when prices rise and beds fill up. Booking hostels in advance does offer peace of mind and some travellers prefer it but in most cases it's not really necessary and many of the cheap places don't have websites and can't be found on booking sites.

That said it is worth doing a bit of research into the accommodation picture before you head to a new town and try to at least find out the street or district where most of the budget places can be found.

I've never really stayed in hostels before. What can I expect?

First things first there are many different types of hostel. The popular destinations in Southeast Asia have several 'party hostels' which are great places to socialise and meet people but aren't the best for getting a good night's sleep. This can be fun at times but there will also be days when you want a more relaxing experience and it's easy enough to find quieter places. Some of the budget hostels are very basic and can cost as little as US$2 per night. As you might expect you don't get many luxuries for that but as a minimum you should always have a bed, electricity and in most cases showers with hot water although even many of the supposedly better places are unreliable in that department.

If you stay in dorms then while you can expect to make travel buddies quickly you will probably find some of your room-mates habits fairly annoying. You don't have to stay in sweaty hostel dorms at every single location to keep your costs down. Often you can find budget hotels, beach bungalows or simple guesthouses that have very cheap private rooms for well under $10 per night.

All hostels should provide you with bedsheets but few provide towels. Most will have wifi and lockers for valuables.

What things should and shouldn't you do when staying in dorms?

Make use of the lockers for all your most valuable items (all decent hostels should have them). Be respectful of others especially at night. After 11pm if people are sleeping be quiet and don't turn the lights on. Not everyone wants to party every night so use a flashlight or the light on your phone to guide you. Many people ignore this even in the early hours of the morning. It's very rude and inconsiderate.

If you get lucky, please don't have sex in a dorm (for a few dollars extra you can get a private room!). This should be obvious but again there are those that think it's totally cool to do it in a room full of strangers. Try not to spend ages in the bathroom or shower if there is only one or two and there are lots of people in the hostel. While it may take you hours to get ready at home, you will need to quickly scale this down in Southeast Asia and if you can't then fork out for a private room with an en-suite.

Is it better to travel alone or with friends?

People are different and solo travel isn't for everyone but most who take the plunge and try it prefer it. You get complete freedom to decide where you go and what you do and it becomes entirely your trip, your adventure. You're also more likely to make new friends and meet people from other countries than you would if you were travelling with your friend or boyfriend/girlfriend.

Travelling with a friend or partner is fine provided you are used to spending lots of time in each other's company or are confident that you will get on fine. Consider splitting up for parts of your trip if you start to get on the nerves of your companion or have different priorities in terms of where you want to go.

I'm travelling alone. How do I meet other travellers?

By far the best place to do this is your hostel. Chances are many if not the majority of folks will be doing a similar thing to you and will be equally eager to make travel buddies. Staying in a dorm rather than getting your own room also increases your chances of making friends and the majority of travel friendships begin there. Other good ways to meet people are to do organised trips or to hang out in traveller bars or cafes.

If you're very anxious about travelling alone then there are a few tour companies that offer 'backpacking tours' where you will travel with a group of other travellers. Included in the price are a load of activities and accommodation in each place. It's a good way to meet people and takes away some of the hassle of sorting things out even if it's likely to work out much more expensive and takes away a lot of your freedom to alter the course of your trip.

The budget seems very low. Is it really possible to get by on as little as $20 a day?

Yes it is quite easy to do but only if you're prepared to become a real shoestring traveller! This means staying in occasionally cramped places, travelling on bumpy and unreliable buses and trains and not eating and drinking in fancy bars or restaurants. The budget allows for a little excess every now and then but not every day. In truth most travellers in this part of the world spend more than that but if you are an experienced budget traveller it's by no means impossible to get by on the figures we have quoted.

Have you got any money saving tips for travelling on a shoestring?

The best advice really is to think like a local if you want to keep costs down to a minimum. Many people in Southeast Asia survive on just a few dollars a day and so theoretically can you.

Constantly ask yourself, where would a local eat? How would a local travel? etc. Sure it's not as easy when you don't speak the language and being foreign, some people will treat you as a walking dollar sign and make blatant attempts to overcharge you. The more you travel and the more you get to understand Southeast Asian ways of life, the easier it will become.

Often just a short walk away from the main tourist areas you will find restaurants, bars and rooms costing a fraction of the price of those in the main travel hotspots. Many towns in Southeast Asia have backpacker districts or streets which are full of cheap options but if you're on a really tight budget you can usually find an even better deal in the side-streets around it.

How do I arrange transport between one town and the next?

This varies from country to country but it's almost always cheaper to book tickets directly yourself at the bus/train station rather than through a travel agency of which there are plenty. Generally speaking don't trust those guys as their main concern is making money out of you and often they are comfortable with blindly lying to do so. If you ask for information about trains and buses they will probably try to convince you that the only place to book is in their office.

It's rare that you will need to book tickets in advance but always arrive with some time to spare before your bus or train is supposed to depart. Ask the staff in your hostel for bus, train and boat times.

Is Southeast Asia dangerous?

Parts of the bigger cities and small areas of Thailand, Indonesia, Burma and The Philippines have a dangerous reputation but those areas are pretty easy to avoid. For the most part, they are well away from the typical travel hotspots in any case and whatever your national media may try and tell you, Southeast Asia is predominantly a safe place to travel. Mindanao island in the Philippines (Cagayan de Oro is located here) is one place where governments often advise against travel to, so you should check the current situation before heading there.

You may also have read a lot of stories about the Philippines, which is waging a brutal war on drugs, lately. That shouldn't put you off going but clearly you should be sensible and speak to hostel staff and other travellers to see if there are any major no-go areas. Also and fairly obviously it's not advisable to get involved in drugs and you should respect local laws. The Thai police have also started to crack down on drug offences lately and it's not uncommon for foreigners to be stopped in the street and searched for no apparent reason, particularly around the Khao San Road in Bangkok. Even though they are widely available, penalties for drug offences in Southeast Asia can be very severe.

In terms of violent incidents, Southeast Asians are typically a very peaceful bunch and much less likely to get aggressive or start trouble than your average drunk at 3am in your homeland. However understandably they are sensitive to anyone who insults their culture or behaves in a completely inappropriate way in their country. They put up with a lot more nonsense from foreigners in their countries than they perhaps should so provided you are respectful you should have a trouble-free trip.

There are more nuisances than real dangers. Mild over-charging of foreigners is not uncommon all over the region and this is annoying but it's not worth getting into a fight over small amounts of money. Be wary of tuk-tuk and taxi drivers and negotiate a price before getting in or better still demand the use of the meter where there is one. If they tell you it's broken don't believe them.

It's also always a good idea to keep tabs on general current events in the region. The political situation in a few of these countries is often quite unstable and you can never be quite sure what's around the corner. Avoid any street protests or demonstrations and should a major situation develop while you're in a country, respect any curfews that are put in place and head to one of the neighbouring countries at the earliest opportunity.

I'm a girl travelling alone. Is this safe?

Solo female travellers should find it much less intimidating than travelling alone in South America, parts of Europe or India for example. Generally Southeast Asian men aren't anywhere near as forward as their Latin cousins and not as creepy as some of the men that travel on Indian trains and buses. While there is quite a chauvinistic aspect to Southeast Asian culture this isn't usually directed at foreigners and some of the chauvinists actually find opinionated Western women quite intimidating. Provided you follow basic common sense it is one of the safest parts of the world for solo female travel and huge numbers of girls do travel alone.

What about Brunei? What about East Timor?

Okay so truth be told these aren't actually all that frequently asked questions although both are countries in Southeast Asia so they deserve a mention.

The Sultanate of Brunei is a small but extremely wealthy state in Northern Borneo surrounded by Malaysia. It is rich in natural gas hence its wealth. Its highlight is the extravagant Istana Nurul Iman, the world's largest occupied residential palace although overall Brunei doesn't hold much else of great interest for travellers. If you're in that part of Borneo it might be worth a visit but only a short one.

East Timor in total contrast is much more interesting but desperately poor and has suffered a brutal history under Portuguese and Indonesian rule. It only finally gained independence in 2002 after a bloody civil war and UN peacekeepers were withdrawn a couple of years ago indicating that it is becoming safer. Still hardly any travellers come here, put off primarily by its dangerous reputation. Efforts are being made to build a tourism industry and if you come you will be greeted with an enormous amount of curiosity by locals. It's a fabulous destination for scuba diving with some stunning coral reefs and with great mountain and jungles treks it's certainly a destination for adventure travellers.

What's the weather like and what's the best time of year to visit?

The region is home to many separate micro-climates so there's not really a definitively bad or definitively good time to travel in Southeast Asia. You might want to consider the typical weather conditions when deciding where you go and in what order though.

Mainly it is a tropical region with hot and humid conditions year-round although Northern parts do experience summers and winters (at the same time as the rest of the Northern Hemisphere). Hanoi for example can get fairly cool in December or January while mountainous areas tend to be much cooler and fresher.

Equatorial regions including The Philippines, Indonesia, Malaysia and Singapore experience only a dry and a wet season although not necessarily at the same time. The dry season sees temperatures soar above 35 degrees centigrade so some travellers prefer the slightly cooler rainy season.

Typically the most popular time to visit mainland Southeast Asia (north of Malaysia) is November to February when there is lots of sunshine but temperatures are more bearable and there is little rain. March to May is really hot and the rain starts July time but again there are significant variations in different parts of the region.

11) About

11.1 About Funky Guides

Funky Guides is an offshoot of MyFunkyTravel (www.myfunkytravel.com) which offers backpacking tips, advice and articles for regions across the world.

The aim of Funky Guides is to provide cheap guides for budget travellers written by budget travellers who have had real travel experiences as opposed to professional writers. In each one you will find honest advice and suggestions and some practical information that will help planning your trip, and the trip itself go smoothly. We aim to cut down on the information-overload and summarise the most important bits.

They won't tell you where to eat, where to drink, what time to get up, what to think, where to blow your nose or anything like that. It's a mixture of basic but important information that you can easily refer to every now and then, combined with some ideas that may provide you with a little bit of inspiration that will help your trip take shape.

11.2 About this Guide

This guide was published in February 2017 as an e-book and in April 2017 in paperback. It is designed to help budget travellers and first time backpackers plan their trips in Southeast Asia.

The hostels mentioned in Section 3 have not paid anything to be featured here. They merely provide budget accommodation and have received overwhelmingly positive feedback from travellers. In more remote locations where there is less budget choice and fewer travellers a cheap hotel or hostel has been selected although it is harder to verify that they provide a consistently good service.

Likewise other travel companies and websites that are featured, are only there because they provide a useful practical service for backpackers in Southeast Asia or people planning to visit.

If you still have questions about backpacking in Southeast Asia after reading this guide, you can contact - info@myfunkytravel.com. We will try to get back to you as soon as possible although this may take a few weeks at busy times.

To contact the author of this guide write to mark@myfunkytravel.com.

If you found the guide helpful we would really appreciate it if you left a review on Amazon! We hope to produce more guides in the future and update this one but your support is vital.

Credits

The image on the cover of the Khao San Road is via Justin Vidamo – www.flickr.com/photos/21160499@N04/7622971612

It has been cropped slightly and may be re-used under the CC BY 2.0 license - www.creativecommons.org/licenses/by/2.0/

The map of Southeast Asia is via wikicommons - www.wikitravel.org/en/File:Map_of_Southeast_Asia.png

It has been modified slightly and can reused under the CC BY-SA 1.0 license - www.creativecommons.org/licenses/by-sa/1.0/

25960078R00049

Printed in Great Britain
by Amazon